# AN EYE
## FOR
# A TOOTH

# AN EYE FOR A TOOTH

FIVE SHORT STORIES ABOUT JUSTICE

Gordon Planedin

Primix Publishing
East Brunswick Office Evolution
1 Tower Center Boulevard, Ste 1510
East Brunswick, NJ 08816
www.primixpublishing.com
Phone: 1-800-538-5788

© 2025 Gordon Planedin. All rights reserved.

No part of this book may be reproduced, stored in a retrieval system, or transmitted by any means without the written permission of the author.

Published by Primix Publishing: 02/11/2025

ISBN: 979-8-89194-316-2(sc)
ISBN: 979-8-89194-317-9(e)

Library of Congress Control Number: 2024918706

Any people depicted in stock imagery provided by iStock are models, and such images are being used for illustrative purposes only.

Certain stock imagery © iStock.

Because of the dynamic nature of the Internet, any web addresses or links contained in this book may have changed since publication and may no longer be valid. The views expressed in this work are solely those of the author and do not necessarily reflect the views of the publisher, and the publisher hereby disclaims any responsibility for them.

# CONTENTS

Dedication . . . . . . . . . . . . . . . . . . . . . . . . . . . . . . . . . . . . . . . vii

Chapter 1.  Maggie's Turn . . . . . . . . . . . . . . . . . . . . . . . . . . . 1

Chapter 2.  General Jessie. . . . . . . . . . . . . . . . . . . . . . . . . . 12

Chapter 3.  To Kill a Gopher . . . . . . . . . . . . . . . . . . . . . . . 29

Chapter 4.  Wrong House. . . . . . . . . . . . . . . . . . . . . . . . . . 37

Chapter 5.  Old Arthur. . . . . . . . . . . . . . . . . . . . . . . . . . . . 45

# DEDICATION

## TO MY SWEETHEART MARY

This book was made possible due to the help and encouragement of many people and especially the tireless effort of my daughter Karen and grandson Gordon Shaw.

# CHAPTER 1

# MAGGIE'S TURN

I had to knock on the door few times before I hear her respond in a low voice "Who is it?" "It's Matt, Honey."

"Is that you, Mathew?" The voice is a little stronger and sounding hopeful.

"Yes, come unlock the door." Maggie had been a very good looking woman in her youth and though the aging was expected, the haggard appearance was scary.

Whoever had beat her up had done a thorough job and though they must have tried not to damage the face too much she still had a pretty good shiner on her left eye and her lip was still quite swollen, On her left arm was a sling from having been fractured in the beating.

Having heard through the grapevine that she was in trouble, I had come to see for myself On seeing her condition I was filled with a terrible anger and the first impulse was to find the ones who had done this and kill them on the spot.

Upon cooling down the realization came that it would not solve the problem, only create more.

After some lengthy discussion with Maggie, a plan began to form in my mind and I proceeded to implement it.

After I had dialed the number Maggie had given me, I waited for the phone to start ringing.

On the third ring I heard the click of the connection being made and there a low male voice came on the line.

Yeah?"

"Hello, is this Rennie?" I tried to make myself sound nervous and unsure, which wasn't much of a problem since this is not my line of work.

"Rennie who?" The low voice again, cautious.

"Big Rennie, uh, Twichel," I came back with hesitantly. "Who wants him?" some curiosity in the voice this time.

"Uh, well, like, uh. You see he doesn't know me, but like uh. I got some info he might be interested in, like uh, maybe this info could help keep him out of a big jam."

"Hang on."

Then silence, and in the background I could hear the murmur of low voices in consultation.

"You still there, man?"

A different voice now confident, positive, even while still cautious.

"Yes, uh Rennie?"

"Speaking, what's up man?"

"Well, uh, like uh, I live in this older hotel, see, cause it's cheap, and like uh, does the name Maggie Dewitt mean anything to you.

"Maybe, why?" Curious now.

"Well uh, you know things are kinda tough these days, like to make a buck I mean. And like uh, I don't have a job so I was just lying on my bed wondering where I could get some break to pay my rent."

I just put this last in figuring it would explain my reasons for phoning him.

"Go on!" The voice is a little impatient now.

"Well, uh, while I was lying on my bed there, quiet as a mouse, thinking. I hear these voices coming through the wall of the adjoining room."

"Well I like uh wasn't paying too much attention at first and then this woman's voice started getting louder and kinda excited like."

"Then these men's voices started to get louder too."

"Well like uh, you know that if you hold a glass against a wall and press your ear against the bottom you can hear much better, and well with these thin walls and stuff, it don't work too bad.

"Well I didn't have much to do so I stuck the glass against the wall. Just for some fun, see."

"I like, well you can't hear everything clearly but I could catch enough to get a pretty good picture of what was coming off.

I stopped for a few moments to rest and also to give him a chance to build up his curiosity.

"Well, uh, like it seems these guys must be fuzz or something," I carried on with, "cause they want this woman to go to court to testify against Big Rennie."

"Well, like she's really scared and wants no part of it cause she's sure Rennie would have her blown away, just like that."

"So, like, they keep talking and explaining to her, that there's no sweat, like uh, Rennie can't touch her cause they'll stash her away somewhere safe and relocate her with a new ID when it's all over."

"And then, like, to make it even better they tell her that Rennie will be out of circulation for a while, like in the can.

"While listening I get the impression that they have somebody paid off to make sure you're not sprung for a while."

"Yeah, go on man," he prompted when I stopped to rest for a few seconds. No question of curiosity this time.

"And like I couldn't hear exactly but it seems that the reason they want you of the way is mainly, like uh, to give some other dude a chance to take over your whole gig and like this dude is seems is laying out some pretty good bread to these fuzz for them to take you out of the picture."

"And, uh, it also sounded like they've gotten pretty close to someone in your crowd who's gonna be in a position to help push the knife in."

I laid this last one on him to make sure he wouldn't talk to too many people till he knew which way was up.

"OK, If you're leveling with me man what's your name and where can we get in touch with you."

"well, uh like, I stay next door to Maggie and like uh I thought that if this info would help keep these dudes off your back you could maybe slip a few bucks my way." I suggested

"OK, fella. We'll check this out and if it is on the level we'll get back to you, meanwhile, sit tight and keep your lips buttoned."

"Sure, sure." I said.

I figured the one with the low voice had to be George, according to the way Maggie described the setup, so if that was the case everything seemed to be going well so far.

I didn't think it would take them too long to get down to Maggie's, since if my story was true they would have no time to waste in checking it out.

And if what they say about crooks is true then they don't have to much in others and anything possible.

From my vantagepoint on the fire escape I could see quite clearly without too much danger of being observed and it wasn't long before Rennie's while Lexus with George at the wheel pulled slowly up the curb almost across from the hotel.

After sitting there for a few minutes and carefully surveying the area they must have decided it looked okay and since time was short they slowly eased out of the ca and casually strolled across the street.

Maggie had described them quite well and I had no trouble recognizing Rannie

His suit was well tailored from what was obviously very good cloth.

Tall, well-built, long black sideburns and curly black hair, he made and impressive figure and I could easily understand a girl like Maggie being turned on by him.

They slightly built figure beside him, with his pock-marked face didn't look like too much from here, but if what Maggie said was true, then he was the snake to watch.

They had two flights of stairs and a long hall-way to navigate and since I didn't figure them to hurry. I had plenty of time to make it back to Maggie's room before them.

The room was quite bare and basic as rooms go, with a washroom in one corner and a bed in the opposite corner. In the third corner there was a small clothes rack with a curtain drawn across it.

It did not look like much of a hiding place for anyone, which was maybe a plus in some ways, but I had put a small box on the floor and by standing on this my feet were out of sight and by crouching down slightly I was well concealed.

The 12-gauge shotgun, which I had bought two days before and promptly shortened, kept me company on the box, barrel down and on the ready.

I had been waiting on the box for what seemed an awfully long time and I was beginning to sweat and worry when we heard the soft rap on the door.

No answer.

The rap again. Louder now.

"Who is it!" Maggie's voice sounding scared and nervous, which it should be if my story was true.

"Open up." The knuckles rapped again, more insistent this time.

"Who is it?" Maggie, sounding even more scared and nervous, this time if that was possible.

"It's Rennie, Maggie baby I just want to talk to you." "But I'm in bed." The reply almost a whisper.

"Open the door Maggie or I'll take it off its hinges, you know I will". The voice was still soft but now you could sense the menace in it.

Silence, then slowly the creak of the bed-springs and the slow hesitant steps toward the door.

There was the soft click of the latch being released and slowly the door began to swing open into the room. George was through the door almost as soon as it opened his eyes flicking around the room looking for any potential danger to his boss.

We had changed the bulb to one of a smaller wattage and I guess that and the very bareness of the room was enough to lull his suspicions for the necessary time.

Reggie slipped in almost immediately and the door latch clicked softly behind him.

"What do you want?" Maggie, terrified now, slowly staggered back into the bed. One hand going up as if to protect her throat, her eyes wide, her cheeks pale as a ghost.

She played her part to perfection as this strategy worked well enough to divert their attention to her and away from the other side of the room for enough seconds.

This gave me the necessary opportunity to emerge from the closet, the 12- guage barrels in front of me and both hammers cocked. They both started to swing toward me but by then the trap had dosed and it took only one look at the twin gaping barrels of eternity facing them to inspire the utmost, immediate cooperation on their behalf "Fellas, I'm only gonna tell you this one time so maybe you should pay very dose attention."

My voice still a bit shaky but getting firmer as the situation started looking better and better.

"I am a realist and the one thing I know for sure is that if you ever get the drop on me both Maggie and I are dead meat. Well then you can see that I don't have a damn thing to lose so the first wrong move either of you make I will let go with both barrels and they will be scraping you guys off of the wall."

"·What's your game man" This from Rennie, some of the confidence gone from his voice, but his eyes are hard, and his face livid with anger.

"No questions, you'll know soon enough," my voice is quite firm now, strange what a transformation a 12-guage in your hands makes in a man.

After I had them spread-eagled against the wall, Maggie, very carefully, and keeping herself in the clear, relieved George of his 32 Special and also his switchblade knife and the keys to the car.

Not surprisingly Rennie was clean except for about $450 in cash and a nice gold ring on his finger and when we finished he was even cleaner than that.

That chore taken care of I proceeded to instruct them on our next move.

As per instructions we slowly proceeded out of the hotel, across the street to Rennie's car, the 12-guage concealed under my light overcoat and the 32 special in Maggie's pocket.

Once there, we carefully proceeded to get in. Maggie first, into the back with 32 cradled in her lap then George into the driver's seat with Rennie beside him.

It was a little tricky getting into the seat behind George but since there weren't many people around I managed quite well.

After everyone was settled in Maggie passed the keys to George and I proceeded to give him instructions for our trip, reminding him that the barrels of the shotgun were against the back of the seat and that if any problems developed he was one person who wouldn't care how they were resolved.

I must compliment Rennie on his choice of George as his right hand, cause, knowing it was useless to try to make any play at this time he proceeded to chauffeur us very competently through the traffic and onto the exit where we were soon on the highway heading out of the city.

It took us less than an hour to exit out onto the side road and then it was only three or four miles till we turned onto the private road and over the hills to a small cabin in a clump of trees.

I had rented it less than a week before from an old bachelor who lived in the next county.

Maggie had the keys ready and she went in first, turned on the light and then we ushered our guests inside, and there with the help of a plentiful supply of rope, which I had prepared earlier, we proceeded to render our guests quite harmless.

This taken care of, I then proceeded to enlighten Rennie of the reasons for our actions.

"Rennie, Maggie was my girl once back in a little town we both called home, but she wasn't ready to settle down yet and neither was I so we split and went our separate ways."

"I joined the marines and knocked around for a few years and Maggie came down to the city for some fun and excitement."

"Not your fault, okay."

"Then she met you and you made the big moves and in no time you had her eating out of your hand. Partly your fault."

"Then you started her on drugs, soft ones at first and then soon she was going for everything. Mostly your fault."

"She didn't find out until too late that you were working a string of girls and by then you had her so strung out she had to go too. All your fault."

"Then in one of her saner moments she realized where this would all have to end and so she hung on to some of the money and tried to get out of town and this rat race."

"You sent George after her and when he brought her back he beat her up bad. Your fault and George's."

"Well she somehow managed to get hold of me, in desperation and told me of her problems and so I came." "Rennie, you took her decency, her pride and her self-respect and caused her a lot of pain, so you owe her big time."

"Okay, so you can't give them back, but you're a big time operator and I figured you must have a good chunk stashed away someplace and we want this, all of it."

"I figure this will give her a nest egg to go somewhere and start over and maybe make a life for herself."

"Okay, you know yourself that we don't have much time before someone starts looking for you so it is best for you to cooperate to help us get your stash."

"Do that and once we're in the dear we'll phone someone and tell them where they can find you and cut you free."

All the while Rennie' taking this in, I notice that somehow he don't look so suave and debonair anymore, in fact he keeps licking his lips every so often.

George just sits there not saying a damn word, only when you look at his eyes they're kinda cold and glassy looking, like a rattlesnake's.

Well I hadn't really figured, Rennie's just up and lay out all his bread that easy so I had an incentive plan figured out especially for him.

I brought out the single bitted axe from the woodshed out back and without further ado I used the blunt end of it to smash some of the toes in his right foot with one smooth stroke right through the shine of his beautiful shoe.

The screech he let out made me glad that there were no neighbors around for miles.

I cracked a beer for Maggie and me and we sipped away while we waited for him to calm down.

When he had slowed down to a whimper I gave him another chance to cooperate.

As he still seemed a little hesitant I gave the toes on his left foot a generous whack with the same tool taking care of some of the toe bones on that side.

I cracked a couple more beers for us and we sipped away for another short while.

When he had next quieted down I could see the pain and fear in his eyes as the realization of his predicament settled in.

After I explained to him the number of bones left in his body I could still work on, he couldn't start talking fast enough.

As I had figured he didn't trust banks or safety deposit boxes so he had a nice little wall safe built into the wall behind the fridge in his apartment.

He didn't seem to mind at all giving me the combination to the safe and since we already had keys to his apartment it wasn't long before Maggie was on her way.

While she was gone I proceeded to occupy myself with a few chores I had planned and really the time passed by quite nicely..

A little over two hours later my cell phone started ringing and I answered. I was assured that everything had gone well and that she was on her way back.

The sun was just getting ready to break over the horizon when she pulled back into the yard but the smile on her face put the sunlight to shame.

When we went through the stacks of green in her bag we found we had well over 16 thousand so with what he had taken from Rennie and George we were pushing 17 thou. Not bad for a couple of days of work.

Meanwhile, I had gotten our gear stacked by the rear door so it didn't take long to load it into the car especially since Rennie and George weren't in the way.

While she'd been gone I had dug a narrow trench down a couple of feet in a sandy patch between a couple of bushes till it was wide enough and deep enough to fit them both in.

I had given each of them a good thump on the head with the blunt end of the axe as a going away present and after that they seemed delighted with their new digs.

I had no way of knowing if they were dead or not but I figured they had helped keep a lot of good people in a kind of living death so I guess things kinda even up. I had covered the trench fairly good in the nighttime but with daylight I was able to fine-tune it and after scattering some leaves and branches on it the site looked very natural.

When I had paid the owner of the cabin for a months rent I'd told him that I'd probably be moving out some time sooner and that if I didn't get to see him I would lock the doors and leave the keys inside for him.

We pulled into Seattle towards evening, and after a couple of drinks and a fine meal in a nice motel on the outskirts we packed it in and got ourselves a much-needed rest.

Early in the morning we drove downtown to a location near a motor vehicle branch office where Maggie went in and explained to the clerk that being interested in purchasing a vehicle privately, she wanted to check to see if there were any liens or charges against it.

Well, $11 and an hour and a half later we had a call back to inform us that it was dear and paid for.

By that time I had practiced doing Rennie's signature to the stage where he would have had trouble telling the real one from the fake himself.

Explaining to the used car dealer that having won the car in a high stakes poker game, I wanted to convert it into cash without any unnecessary paperwork.

Having a signed copy of a vehicle transfer for the car and the driver's license number now on it the salesman proceeded to check with the M.V.B. for liens, etc.

Coming back with a dean check we proceeded to negotiate and the dealer, who, since he knew we wanted cash offered only 6,500 which we all knew was quite a few thousand below its value.

Some negotiating brought this to 6,800 which he proceeded to obtain for us.

While I had been concluding the deal Maggie had been on the blower and by this time had arranged for two tickets on a Pan Am flight leaving for Hawaii early that evening.

As the plane cleared the airport and slowly started to swing to the southwest, we relaxed in our seats with our drinks in hand as we contemplated our future.

Not being spend thrifts we figured that we should be able to find a place to rent at an acceptable price, and relax and enjoy life for awhile and then if we started to run short we could always come back to the mainland and find more operators like Rennie to milk.

# CHAPTER 2

# GENERAL JESSIE

Time was the enemy. She seemed to have almost vanished into thin air and when her mother and father were sure that something was wrong the Sheriff would do nothing worthwhile at all. Sure, be alerted whoever was on patrol to keep an eye out for her but would go no further. "She might be out riding with some of her friends or visiting someone." Even when they tried to explain to him that she had said she would only be gone for about half an hour and that she was very conscientious about informing them of any change of plans, and that they had phoned around to everyone they could think of and no one knew anything of her whereabouts.

Morning came and with it the firm conviction that something was terribly wrong and some immediate action should be taken. Marysville is a little town in the Northeast corner of Oregon State with a population of about 1200 people. An economy of farming and ranching, and combined with a small leather factory that employed about 60 people kept the town, if not overly prosperous, at least comfortably secure. Highway 26, which runs through our town, was fronted on both sides by a variety of small businesses as well. as a small burger stand.

The highway running east of the burger stand has a small dog leg, where it makes a right turn, then straight for two blocks, which is where the factory stands, then turns left again to continue on the 2 blocks straight ahead and then instead of turning left again to continue east towards the Madras.

The side walk on the south side of the highway is the path that Jenny took on her way home from the burger stand and the witnesses remembered her turning right at the corner, where she would continue on the 2 blocks straight ahead and then instead of turning left with the highway, she would normally walk another block and a half straight ahead and she would be home. She did not reach home.

By the afternoon of the following day, Sheriff Bigley finally relented and after starting to share the parents concern's somewhat, put out an APB, with her picture and description.

Jenny was on the last semester in her grade 12 class, near the top of the class and a very thoughtful and considerate daughter and a pleasure to everyone who came into contact with her. Her brother Chris, who was 2 years older, had graduated and was knocking around in Portland trying to find himself and decide on a career. The oldest boy, Jessie 23, was stationed with a U.S Marine Group not too far away.

Even before the APB's were issued the parents had contacted them both and having been very close to their sister, they had been assured the boys would make it home as soon as possible to help with the search.

During the process of searching the surrounding area it came to their attention that 6 or 7 members of a bike gang had cruised through town heading east about the time Jenny disappeared. No one had paid too much attention to them because they often cruised through town on their way to a hangout they had some miles further east near the warm spring's area, and had not caused any problems locally.

The next afternoon, with the search still fruitless, the parents received a call from a woman who would not give them her name but she said that when she saw the bikers go by a few miles east of town she thought it strange that one of the bikers, instead of having his passenger in the seat behind him had the passenger in the front of him. The passenger was wearing a heavy winter jacket, and no helmet and she had assumed it to be a female because of the long blond hair-streaming out behind, When they passed this information on to Sheriff Bigley. He discounted it because he said if the caller would not provide her name the information could not be considered reliable.

Thankfully the boys both showed up later that day, and that evening the family thrashed out the details of what they knew and also other prospects. The boys, loading their sleeping bags and other essentials onto Jesse's green club cab, were off at daylight to initiate their own search, with the assurance that they would keep in contact as necessary.

The information provided by the unidentified caller seemed to interest Jessie and since nothing else was working out they decided to check out that lead. About an hour's drive east on 26, at a junction with Prairie Road, there was an establishment, which was a combination restaurant, mini market and gas bar called Ernie's place. According to the locals, a few miles down Prairie Road at the base of the mountain was where the biker gang had their hangout.

Not wanting to attract too much attention, the boys cruised down on Prairie Road at a normal rate of speed with their eyes trying to take in everything they could. About 6 ⅝ miles down on Prairie Road they saw a dirt road leading up into a draw and it looked like a lot of bike tracks on the road. They were able to get glimpses of some building a ways up the draw but the scary part was that even at that distance you could hear the baying of what sounded like some very unfriendly dogs. It was very troubling in that even if they could be sure that Jenny was being held captive in that stronghold it would take a small army to liberate her and they could not count on anyone helping them without proof that Jenny was in fact inside.

Feeling frustrated they decided to drop into Ernie's for a quick burger before carrying on back to Marysville. On the way back to Ernie's they spotted a trail heading down to a creek. Jesse drove the truck down and they found what was probably a favourite summertime spot. There was a nice grassy meadow leading down to a sandy beach on the water.

A variety of small bushes framed it from both sides leaving an opening to the water of about 60 feet. To add to the attractiveness of the spot was the fact that someone had left a simple, basic, but well made picnic table in the area along one side.

They were most of their way through their burger and coffee when their big break came. At first it sounded like some thunder back in the hills but soon they realized it was the sound of motorcycles coming closer. Sitting in a corner booth they had a very good view of the pumps and sure enough, within a couple of minutes eight bikers pulled up to the pumps to fuel up. Since they had pulled in from Prairie Road it was safe to assume that they were members of that gang.

That biker that pulled in first was a tallish grey haired individual, pockmarked face and somewhat stopped in the back and from his actions they assumed he was the head honcho. When the gang had fuelled up they pulled out onto 26 heading west except for one of them who pulled around behind the building and parked. A few minutes later he was entering the restaurant with his saddlebags over his arm. As he passed the girl at the cash he greeted her and they heard her response as a "Hi Shorty, how are you doing?" He grunted and proceeded to wander down to the grocery section giving the distinct impression that he was shopping for some supplies for the camp.

Their bill was on the table for about $12.50 so Jesse laid fourteen dollars on top of it, jerking his head towards the door and they proceeded to quietly exit the place. They circled the building to the parking area and sure enough there was the cycle parked about thirty feet from the pick-up. Jesse had the plan laid out quickly so that when Shorty came around to his bike they were ready.

Shorty was just finishing strapping his bags to the bike when Jesse strolled up to him and with a cigarette in his mouth, asked "Got a light?" Shorty was starting to give him some sarcastic answer when Jesse, who was now only a few feet from him, opened up his jacket and then Shorty could see the army issue revolver in his waistband and Jesse's hand on the pistol butt.

He was starting to mutter something when he was cut off with a sharp command, "Shut your face and listen good or you won't be around to have any supper tonight". He followed instructions well and they quickly had him by the passenger side of the pickup and having him remove his leather jacket. Then it was face down on the floor behind the front seat; they had him bring his hands to the back so they were able to inactivate him in short order. They were fortunate that the back of the building was blank with no windows so there was total privacy for them.

The leather jacket was somewhat snug for Jesse but he managed to get it on okay. With a "Give me a minute or two start and then meet me at the picnic table by the river", he was on the bike. Having driven quite a few of his buddies bikes through his teens he had no trouble firing up and in seconds he had rounded the corner and was cruising down Prairie Road back towards the hangout. Checking to make sure that Shorty was secure, Chris, with the revolver on the seat beside him, proceeded to pull out of the parking lot following his brother. At the picnic area they proceeded to sit Shorty on one side of the table with his legs straddling the seat and then tied his feet together with a short piece of poly rope.

Their communication was short and to the point, they knew their sister was a captive at the biker's camp and their only concern was to obtain her release and then they would be on their way. When Shorty explained that she was there with one more biker and two broads the plan became simple. Shorty was to use their cell phone to call the camp and have the other fellow bring her down on the car they had there.

Shorty was assured if anything went wrong there would not be any tomorrow for him. When they answered at the camp Shorty informed the other guy that Weasel (that was the name of the big Kahoona) was concerned that there were fuzz checking around and that he wanted to relocate Jenny to a safer place.

"Put her in the back seat of the Chevy with the wrap's on her hands and feet and cover her with a blanket and then meet me at the swimming hole" was the advice. While they were waiting for the next move they put Shorty through a third degree regarding the gang and where the rest of them were off to.& suspected, they were dealing in drugs and the rest of the gang were off to.

Portland to buy another. The gang would drive to within a few miles of Portland where they would camp over at their regular spot and then the next morning Weasel and another biker would go into town to make their purchase.

With a little "coaxing" Shorty informed them that Weasel had 65 thousand packed into his saddlebags and also he gave them explicit instructions on how to find their camping spot.

When the other biker arrived at the site the scene was all set as there was only Shorty sitting at the table facing toward the car pulling up with a can of beer taken from his saddlebags in his hand and another can for his buddy across from him. The boys had made sure that his pant legs and also the grass that grew around there hid the rope binding his feet so that everything looked casual and normal.

By the time his buddy had settled onto the opposite seat Jesse came strolling around the adjoining hazelnut bush with his revolver in his hand and Chris emerged from the other side with a 30.06 rifle.

He started to lift up, but almost immediately sat back down again. He was quickly herded down to the other side of the bush where he was out of sight, laid face down on the ground and his hands and feet securely tied. Shorty was there to join him in short order and also secured.

When they proceeded to the Chevy they found that Jenny was in fact there on the back seat, securely fastened and gagged. Freeing her, they spent the next few minutes hugging and laughing reassuring her that she was now safe. Then, explaining to her that they were not completely out of the woods yet they helped her get comfy on the back seat of the pickup where they covered her with a blanket to be warm and also out of sight. Chris was instructed to drive the pick up two or three miles up Prarie Road, then turn around and come back. When they pulled out Jesse proceeded to wheel the cycle around the bush where he laid it down beside the bikers. Figuring that Chris should be about ready to turn around by now, Jesse walked back to the bikers with the pistol wrapped in a old jacket he had found in the Chevy he bent over and placing the nuzzle behind Shorty's left ear he pulled the trigger, and then quickly swinging around and to be fair gave the other fellow one of the same.

Not wanting to leave any evidence behind he carried the jacket with him as he went back to the Chevy and starting it he moved it to the far side of the clearing where he parked it, not locking the doors and leaving the keys in the ignition,

When they had first started the whole procedure, Jesse had found some plastic gloves in the toolbox of his pickup and both he and Chris had put them on so as not to leave any fingerprints behind. He had just finished his chores when Chris pulled back into the clearing and threw the jacket into the toolbox he climbed in and they began to roll.

They turned onto 26 heading west towards Marysville and Portland and proceeded to drive in as normal fashion as possible in order to attract as little attention as possible. During the hours drive till they reached home Jesse slowly and patiently explained to his sister that there were some things to be done yet and that they needed her help and co-operation. The boys would park the truck just past their parents house so that they could see her make her way safely to the door but so that the truck was out of view. She was to tell the parents only that some people had dropped her off and had cautioned her about providing any further details as it could cause major problems for the family. Her standard response was to be that it was a long story and that she was tired and did not wish to discuss it any more at this time. She was also to ask her parents to please not inform the authorities of her safe return until the following morning.

Receiving the assurance of her cooperation they soon pulled into town and as it was now dusk they had no problem completing their plan. After watching her through the branches till she was through the door they slowly drove back onto 26 heading further west towards Portland.

During the next run Jesse explained to Chris that his decision to finish the bikers was because of his conviction that as long as any of the gang remained alive neither Jenny nor any of the family could be safe. His further explanation was that he had joined the Marines in order to be able to fight against evil people. "Before we go out into the world to fight evil there, I think we should try to eliminate some of the evil at home", he said,

"This gang not only kidnapped and sexually assaulted Jenny but they are engaged in a trade that destroys many other lives and therefore they should be stopped." he added.

The instructions that Shorty had provided were very good and as soon as they passed the sign which said 1 1•miles to Portland they began to watch for the Exxon Gas Station on their left and finding that one it was easy to spot Willow Drive just past on the left hand side also. Turning on to Willow Drive they watched and as Shorty had described, on the right hand side, about 1/2 a mile down there was the trail branching out through the trees.

They kept on the main road but even driving along at a reasonable speed they could spot glimpses of a bonfire a short way over as they carried on. Spotting a sort of grassy road off on the right side, Jesse slowed down and followed it through a few twists and turns till they were well out of sight from Willow Drive. Parking the pick up on a bit of a clearing they carefully walked back along the bench till within a few hundred yards they were on the edge looking down on the encampment.

Since it was quite dark by now they were able to sit down on a couple of stumps by the edge with an excellent view of the bikers. The gang had quite a nice fire going down below as they sat around on some logs around the fire, with some roasting wieners and smokies and most of them sucking on their beers. Even from this distance you could smell the marijuana as some of them were puffing on their joints.

After surveying the set-up below the boys went back to the pickup and had by a sandwich and beer from their supplies they had "borrowed" from Shorty, since he had no more use of them. They strolled back to Willow Drive then down to where the trail turned off and walking very quietly down the trail toward the fire they were able to plan their strategy for the next day.

Once back at the truck they proceeded to pull out their sleeping bags from the lock box and rolling them out on the bed of the truck they laid down for a few hours of rest. They were up about an hour before sunup and after a quick bite they began to prepare for a proper wake up call for the bikers.

Chris, taking with him a small coil of% poly rope and Jesse's revolver, as well as one of the handsets of a small 2-way intercom that Jesse always used during hunting, headed back down Willow Drive to the trail· and to spot they had preselected just hours before. In the meantime, Jesse had taken with him the 30-06 rifle, a few clips of hollow point ammo, a couple of beers, the other handset and an old blanket to lie on.

He slowly worked his way to the most comfortable of the stumps to where he could rest the barrel of the rifle and have total command of site below.

As soon as the shadows started to lighten and visibility was rapidly improving they had their last contact. With the assurance from Chris that his end was done, Jesse informed him that as soon as he felt comfortable with visibility he would commence.

Not too long after the bikers were starting to stir and the first one up, a chubby fellow, leaving his sleeping bag and relieving himself, started a big yawn as he stood facing the hillside. The hollow point slug entered his mouth, pulling a few teeth on the way, and exiting out the back took out part of the back of his head.

Armageddon had arrived for the bikers early, and with a loud bang. There were a few moments of confusion as the rest were trying to come out of their sleep and get hold of what was going on. Those were moments that they didn't have the luxury of wasting. Jesse, having been an excellent shot always, had upon joining the Marines, and his supervisors becoming aware of his prowess with a rifle, been put into a program where they were training people to be marksmen and snipers.

The bikers were like ducks in a barrel and actually were dead in the water as one could say. One person, on climbing out of his bag, did not even try to stand up but tried to crawl away to safety. The slug caught him between the shoulder blades and helped him to get a few feet further in a hurry, where he lay twitching for a while.

The execution proceeded with deadly precision where as soon as someone moved they would quit moving just as quickly. To give Jesse credit, he did a superb job and wasted no ammo and it was basically one bullet per customer.

Through all this time, Weasel, proving the old adage that "rats desert a sinking ship", had headed for his bike a few yards away and with the attitude of a true General, "every man for himself", and not even bothering to put his boots on.

His money belt was draped over the gas tank and jumping on he had the engine roaring in seconds and pulling a sharp circle around the remnants of the fire he headed out on the path to safety. As he came tearing around a small curve, accelerating, he had no way of knowing that Chris had been preparing a welcome especially for him. The previous evening while observing the gang they had been able to identify Weasel's bike, and seeing that it did not have a windshield, had made their plan accordingly. During the half hour before, Chris had taken the heavy polyethylene rope, good for a 7000 pound pull, and winding one end around a skookum tree 4 or 5 times and ending up with a slip knot, had stretched the rope across the path to another good tree almost directly across and looping it a few times around that tree had made the end secure. When Weasel came speeding around the curve he probably spotted the rope at the last second but regardless it was much too late. The rope, just clearing the handlebars, caught him in the chest, and because he was bent way forward on his bike, slid up his chest, dug into his throat, crushing it and snapping his spine in the process of unloading him from his bike. He landed on the ground, flat on his back and a few inches taller than he had been a few seconds earlier.

His bike, meanwhile, with the load removed had gone careening into the heavy brush where it had come to a sudden stop and lay there with the motor silent and the back wheel spinning lazily in the morning sun.

Chris trotted over to Weasel with the revolver in his hand but immediately saw that the weapon was not necessary, Weasel lay there with blood oozing out of his mouth and nose, making some strange guttural sounds but it was obvious that with his windpipe crushed to that degree he would not be making any long term plans.

Trotting over from Weasel towards the bike Chris found the money belt on the ground and a few feet further he was at the bike where it took him no time at all to liberate the saddlebags. Laying them both by one of his anchor trees he proceeded to pull the slipknot and free that end from the tree. Freeing up the other end he was able to coil up the rope in record time. With the coil of rope and the money belt in one hand and the saddlebags in the other he was soon trotting down the path to Willow Drive.

The timing was quite good cause shortly after reaching there he could see Jesse come slowly down the road towards him. He was across the road to the passenger's side and was waiting when Jesse stopped and throwing the rope and saddlebag in the toolbox he climbed into the cab with the money belt and gun in hand as they headed down the road. He proceeded to wrap the gun in an old towel, which was lying on the floor, and carefully slid it under the seat and then he began to unload the money belt.

"Weasel's pretty nice to us" Chris remarked as he counted the take, "There's over eleven hundred dollars here." The divvy went in an amicable fashion, 700 to Jesse since he was paying the shot so far, and the balance Chris stuck into his jean's pocket.

When they stopped to relieve themselves a few miles down the road Chris found some small cks and loaded up the money belt so that he was ready when they crossed a small river shortly before they entered onto Interstate 84 to head east. As Jesse slowed down in the middle of the he was able to fire the money belt into the water below. Having made sure that it was clean of any prints they felt that even if it were found there would be no links to them.

Once back on the road they proceeded at a reasonable speed to be sure to not attract attention, a mile or two above the speed limit, which was the normal innocent driver would do. At first opportunity after entering the freeway they pulled into a self-serve station and while Chris filled up both tanks, money being no problem, Jesse went into the store part and grabbed some buns, cheese and meat slices, ice cubes for their cooler and two dozen cold ones, paying with cash. While at the station Jesse had, scoring a bunch of quarters phoned from the pay phone to the gang headquarters, and talking around the piece of meat in his mouth had delivered a short and striking message to the woman answering the phone, "Just to let you know, honey, the shit has hit the fan and I can give you only one piece of advice, clean out the hangout so that there is nothing left to tie you to any one of the gang, then hit the trail and don't look back before your ass becomes grass!".

"He hung up before the woman even had the chance to respond.

By alternating the driving and since they had enough beer and growlies to sustain them they were soon on 395 north and then some time later on Interstate 90 heading towards Montana. Maintaining a constant speed with no waste of time by mid afternoon they had left Washington crossed Idaho and were in the hills close to Plains, Montana. Being fairly familiar with the area they were soon in a nice meadow next to a stream where they were happy to start a nice bonfire. While having their beer and sandwiches they found a nice area in which to dig and with the aid of a shovel Jesse always kept in the lock box they proceeded to dig some holes. In one of them they buried the 30-06 down about 3 feet to be sure it was never to be discovered. The other hole covered up the saddlebags, after milking them of the 65 thousand that Shorty had said would be in them for the purchase of more drugs.

The loot, neatly bundled in stacks of 20s, 50s and hundreds was carefully stacked in a clean burlap sack which Jesse had bought on one of their infrequent stops and then it was put into a plastic bag and stored into a very snug place between the gas tank and the frame where they were sure it would not only ride securely but more importantly would be very hard to spot.

Having burned the gloves, the jacket from Chevy, ropes and anything else which they thought could be used as evidence they checked into a motel not far from Plains, Montana explaining to the lady clerk that having spent the night before in sleeping bags in the wilderness they wanted a good hot bath and some sleep before hitting the road. After checking in at the motel the boys had a couple of pizzas delivered to their room and still having a fair stock of beer they sat back to relax and watch the news.

They found it hard to believe the amount of coverage that was generated by their involvement with the bikers. One prominent national TV station was of the opinion that it was a gang war between rival drug dealers and concerned that innocent people could get hurt. Their final comment was that the group that was responsible was obviously very professional in that field.

The most interesting report came from some local news media where the reporter covering the event was suggesting that it could be a vigilante group. It seems that in the spring two teenage girls had been raped and beaten about the time the bikers had camped in that area and although the girls were too terrified to testify, the general feeling was that it had been the bikers. With the general public nation-wide becoming increasingly concerned that the legal system was useless when it came to protecting the common people, there was the ever growing murmur that if you wanted to see justice done you should get off your ass and make sure yourself that it in fact gets done.

He went a step further in his comments in that unless there were major changes soon it was probably the only option left for justice to prevail.

Shortly after their meal, Jesse phoned the folks after being reassured that Jenny was fine and informed them that they had had a couple of restful days in Montana and would be heading back in the morning.

They pulled into Marysville in the early afternoon and after having a few pleasant hours with the family they informed the folks_ that Jesse, having taken compassionate leave from the base should head back there and Chris wanted a ride to the bus station as he had job interviews he should attend back home.

Throughout their youth, the boys, having to find some secure place for their "valuables", girlie books, etc. had very ingeniously remodeled a plank in their parents storage shed so that unless you knew it was hinged and the process to make it move, was safer than Fort Knox.

During a short span of the time when they were with their folks, Chris having a prior arrangement with Jesse, had taken the nest egg from the pickup and deposited it in Fort Knox. During their long drives they had ample opportunity to discuss the future and the consensus was that although the money would remain basically intact for now, it was in fact a legacy from "Weasel and Company" towards the betterment of the family in the years to come.

Before leaving that afternoon the boys had some very private moments with their sister during which time she had commented that she had been watching the news about the happenings at Portland and her feelings towards those events. She said that when she heard the news about Weasel and the gang being gone it was like a stone being lifted from her chest and strangely she felt clean once again. Her hug with Jesse on his departure was very emotional as she whispered in his ear, "Whoever removed them from us made me feel free once again, thank you".

Parting from Chris, having been very close and now having to let go again, they stood there with tears streaming down their faces. She had only one comment; "Thank God I have brothers like you and Jesse." And then the boys were gone.

There was a considerable discussion regarding their fallout with Dan Bigley. He was not satisfied with their explanation that the reason they had not informed him about Jenny's return till early next morning was because Jenny was totally bagged out and needed rest and that any search crews would not be dispatched till later in the morning.

When questioned about the brothers, the folks had informed him that on phoning home the night before and being told that Jenny was home, tired and asleep they had decided to take a couple of days to cruise down to Montana to check out a few future hunting areas.

Bigley's contact with the family next morning was to him very unsatisfactory, being informed that Jenny still had no comment even if she had to go to jail, the boys had carried on, Jesse having to report back to the base and Chris having his own personal problems.

It was interesting to note that the Chevy which had been abandoned by the swimming hole had been discovered by some local youth and finding the keys in the ignition and a tank 3/4 full of gas had decided that it was a gift from above and proceeded to run it into the ground.

The bodies of Shorty and his bud were not discovered for two weeks till a hunter strolling along the creek chanced upon them. By this time the original outburst of publicity regarding the reckoning had basically petered out so it was a slow process in trying to establish ties to the other episode.

However to Bigley the picture was very clear and so he was waiting at City Hall when the mayor arrived and could hardly contain himself till he got the mayor off to the side where they had some privacy to tell him the whole story. "It all fits together like a glove" he said. "The. bikers grabbed Jenny and had her at their camp. I don't know how her brothers managed it" he carried on," but they obviously not only rescued their sister but also shot the two bikers in the process. Having got all the necessary info from those two, they had followed the gang and wiped them out. Leaving there in the early morning the boys had lots of time to make it to Montana to establish their alibis. I checked into Jesse at the Marine Base (very discretely) and found out that he was a crack shot with a rifle which could explain how those bikers could all be killed in a short time with a minimum of shots fired. I think we should talk to the prosecutor about some search warrants and do some arresting. "

Mayor Sneddon had been listening to this barrage of talk while slowly shaking his head from side to side. "Biggy, I would like you to do me a few favors, first give your head a big shake, then I want you to do some thinking along this line. The massacre happened two weeks ago and to this date I have not heard of any evidence worth shit having been discovered. The opinion of basically everyone concerned is that the perpetrators not only planned this well but also executed it even better. If in fact Jesse and Chris pulled this two weeks ago and left nothing there, then assured that they would have deaned up the minor stuff since. So the calibre of the gun that was used to shoot the two bikers at the swimming hole is the same as the revolvers issued by Marine Corp., so what."

"Jesse has been back at the base for a week and a half, and since it's obvious he is no fool, would have switched his revolver with any of possibly hundreds of similar guns in the first day or two upon returning.

If you think we are going to obtain a search warrant to check out the hundreds of revolvers at the base for a possible match, forget it! They would run us off the base. Think much further ahead and realize what would happen that, if, by some chance, we could come up with some evidence, circumstantial or whatever, and managed to arrest these boys and bring them to trial. There would be no prospect of finding a jury of 12 normal people whom even if they believed in their heart of hearts that the boys had if fact done the deed would be willing to bring in a verdict of guilty. Rather, they would regard the boys as heroes."

"The sad part is the aftermath. I am up for reelection as mayor in the spring and I will tell you that after trying to punish these fine local boys in the courts my name would be mud. The opposition would be able to run Mr. Johnston's pig against me and I'll tell you for true the pig would win. I would also like to remind you that it was this office that got you your position and that after the election, without question, you would be kicking horse turds down the road yourself'

"So follow my advice and take these speculations of yours and flush them down the toilet and do not under any circumstances share them with anyone, not even your wife. 1be big boys in Portland have the expertise, the money and the time to sort this thing out and if any one comes around trying to tie Jenny to this mess, just tell them that to the best of our knowledge she had taken off for a few days with some friends she had met and sobering up had decided to come home."

Meanwhile, Jenny, realising that she in spite of having had a very scary and dangerous situation, had come out fairly well because in the few days she was a captive she had been Weasel's exclusive and that surely after the novelty wore off he would start to share her and she would have had to pull the train. She finished high school, and with the assurance from her brothers of adequate funding, entered college for a career in youth counselling.

Chris, meanwhile, having had a taste of life, and "finding himself, had assured the folks that in the Fall he would be entering into a career in the law profession.

Jesse, after some thought and reliving the experience in his mind time and time again, decided he should stay with the military, where using his varied actual experience, and studying might someday become an officer with possibly more than two people under his command.

# CHAPTER 3

# TO KILL A GOPHER

From the beginning, I was puzzled by the expression on her face. There was fear, of course surprise, a realization of impending doom, but there was some-other substance I could not quite lay my finger on.

She was still lying on her bed, her neck twisted sideways because of the pressure of the pillow which had been forced upon her face which had denied her any further life.

There were signs of a breakage of glass, consistent with someone breaking a section of the outside window in order to open it to gain access to the room. There were some faint footprints from the outside window to her bed to support the conclusion that someone breaking in had been confronted by her, and in desperation, smothered her.

Otherwise the suite seemed fairly well undisturbed other than the dresser drawer having been searched and milked clean.

The investigation did not take too long, and the obvious conclusion was that the intruder, having been surprised, had suffocated her in order to make his escape. The main bothersome fact to Martha and I was that whoever killed Liz had not bothered to steal her VCR or other small items which were easier to dispose of but had taken her necklace and earrings, and with her ears being pierced would have taken more time and also they would be easier to identify, and therefore harder to sell.

The victim, Liz, Elizabeth Adele Hansard, Martha Sedgewick, both widowed, and myself were fortunate tenants in a seniors housing project, that, while being within a few blocks of a shopping area, was far enough to the side of a main thoroughfare to provide *us* with a surprisingly quiet place. There were approximately forty tenants in the complex but for some reason the three of *us* had become, in a very short time, the best of friends.

Myself, having grown up in the Prairies during the depression had, of necessity, become a jack of all trades early on, since there was always something on the farm that needed fixing. When I was about eleven years old I entered into an agreement with the manager of our local general store to shoot some gophers that were a problem to the grain farmers in our area. He had some cages in back of the store where he was raising mink for the furs, and the gophers provided *him* with. a supply of fresh meat. With an almost endless supply of gophers I had a small but dependable source of income for the summer (2 gophers for 5 cents) which may not seem like big money now, but considering that my old man worked at a neighboring farm, 6 days a week for only 30 dollars a month, it was a nice bit of coin.

To make things more interesting I had my buddies anxious to get involved, and when one of them brought along a single shot 22-calibre pistol, we were in our glory as we, imagining ourselves as a Roy Rogers type, tried to shoot the gophers straight from the hip.

Then when I was fourteen years old and we had the local electrician installing some lighting on our farm I had the opportunity to provide *him* with some help and save my father some bucks.

Growing up and getting married to Roseannne came along, then 3 children, 2 boys and a girl and the usual ups and downs of a normal family life. Life was beautiful as the children grew up, married and then started having children of their own.

Tragedy struck without warning. My wife of 37 years developed cancer in her lungs, and then some eight short months later Rosie was gone. I was at a total loss for some time and was fortunate that the family took care of basically everything that had to be done for quite some time. In the end there was either the option of living with some of the family or a new start in this care home, and at 62 years old I decided there were far too many memories of Rosie around, and not wanting to be a burden to any part of the family, I decided to try the care home and play it from there.

The first few weeks were not that great but after meeting Lizzie first, then Martha and when they started to take care of me as someone would a lost stray dog, life started to improve.

The original landlord, god bless his soul, had been a wonderful person who built this place (with a hefty mortgage) with the thought in mind it could be an excellent place for retiring seniors and he was absolutely right. He had also provided a small area in the rec. room just outside his small office and equipped it with a table chairs, a small electric stove and some shelving so that the tenants could bring their goodies and sit and socialize and do their tea and cookies bit. Before long, Liz, Martha and I would spend time together there having our tea, playing a variety of games and just being able to relax and discuss problems and enjoy whatever was left of our lives.

When our landlord passed away due to an early heart attack, he left the complex to his daughter, who had two boys from an earlier failed marriage. Her current boyfriend, Benjamin Sidly was an opportunist who; perceiving the potential, proposed to, and married the girl almost before the funeral services were over.

His arrival on the scene was not a happy occasion, since he proceeded to raise rents and increase restrictions on a regular basis.

He was also very strict with the boys and very demanding of them, and later on there were suggestions that he had become abusive to his wife.

The truth of the whole terrible incident started becoming clearer and clearer after a strange discovery I made in his office a few days later.

I had been in the process of paying my rent when there was a sudden interruption from outside.

It seems his stepsons had been playing catch in the courtyard when an errant ball broke a small pane of glass in one of the windows.

He stormed out of the office in a rage, leaving me there to await his return. In trying to occupy my time while waiting for him to return, I went over to the wall of the office adjoining the living area and tried to straighten the picture hanging on the wall.

Unable to move it, I put a little pressure on it thinking it was stuck to the wall. To my surprise it lifted but only on the bottom side. Then by further lifting I found that it was hinged on top and opened up as a lid. Fastened to the back of it was a piece of 3" thick Styrofoam which fit exactly into the opening in the wall.

Then I discovered that on the opposite side of the opening was a grill, which was directly over the area in the living room where Benjamin had set out the tea table, and a small hot plate.

Standing at that grill I could clearly hear the conversations of two of the tenants of the residence who were then having their cups of tea. The stark realization crept over me that this whole setup had been engineered by him to enable him to spy on the tenants and know their every move.

My mind went back to the time a few weeks back when Martha and Liz and I had been sitting together and she had expressed concern with the problem of money shortage and had mentioned that she was thinking of having to sell her necklace and earrings in order to keep going and she also had mentioned their potential value. The little known fact was that they had been given to her by her husband as a gift on their 40th anniversary and although they were simply cut they were worth about $4,000.00 at today's prices, she had said.

If Benjamin had been at his spy station, he would have known every detail of that situation. I carefully closed the lid and vacated the room, my mind boggled down with too many scenarios.

Martha and I, out on a bench on the lawn, secure from spies' discussed this situation at considerable length.

There had been rumors that Benjie was into cocaine and was having money problems, which considering the fact that he had a pass key to every apartment, could explain the increasing number of people who seemed to have misplaced money and valuables which never seem to be found.

The inescapable conclusion was that, knowing she might soon sell that valuable set, he had let himself into her room knowing that he would have to kill her in order to obtain the set.

This put the last piece of the puzzle in place regarding the expression of her face: recognition.

The bottom line is that knowing this beyond a reasonable doubt in our minds was not enough. The police had made a conclusion and there was no substantial evidence to try to change their minds.

It soon became obvious to us that if justice were to be done that it would have to be left to Martha and I to do it.

In the ensuing weeks and months, a plan began to formulate, and we proceeded to make the necessary preparations to carry it out. I purchased a cheap motion detector light fixture for the outside light of my suite and replaced the existing fixture, replacing the bulb with one that was burned out.

Next, I drilled a very small hole through the wall opposite the fixture just large enough to fish the cable from a light extension cord through it. I had cut the male cap off the end and with the switch shut off, and the help of the wiring diagram, I spliced the cord into the fixture so that any movement in the entryway would energize cord.

Then with the aid of duct tape, I was able to connect and secure other extensions to create a path to my lamp at my bedside.

The installation was done very neatly so as to be hardly noticeable and when it was complete, the lamp at my bedside would alert me of any movement at the front door.

Over the next few days I managed to obtain a permit to purchase a small 22-calibre pistol and a box of high-powered 22-calibre bullets. The recent tragedy at the apartments made this process much easier.

In my younger days I had been quite familiar with guns and having fired a 22-calibre pistol many times, I was confident I would have no trouble in that regard.

With that part of the preparations complete, we were ready to go on to step No. 2 of the plan, and when we knew Benjamin was in the office, we sat down with Martha to engage in our prepared conversation.

"But why do you want to give up that much of your saving," Martha asked.

"Well, my grandson is ready to go to college, "1 replied. "But I know he is short of money and is considering sidelining his education to go out and earn some. I don't want him to have to do this and since I was going to leave $6,000 of my money towards his education then I think it's better that I do this now and not wait till after I drop."

"What does his father think of this," she asked.

"No one even knows that I have this money as was saving this as a surprise," I replied.

Throughout the conversation I was sure that I could detect a slightly different flow of air around us and I was quite sure we were being monitored.

"When is your grandson coming to see you?" her question. "Ryan should be here on Sunday afternoon which is the day after tomorrow cause I asked him to come to see me, and he treats his grandpa very well."

"He has no idea of what is to come so it should be some happy times."

"Oh, how have you been sleeping lately," her concern about my latest problems.

"I acquired some of that Sominex a few days ago," I replied. "So that as soon as the headline news are over at 10, I take a couple and by 11, I'm out for the night," I assured her.

We were not sure how Benjie would take this, but with the fact that he always needed money and that the window of opportunity was small the prospects ever good.

I went to bed that night with a cover over the bed lamp so that only I would be aware of it coming on. My pistol on the dresser and my newest acquisition, a 500,000-candlepower halogen flashlight right beside it and a prayer on my lips.

I had had a nice light lunch and I managed to doze off a couple of time till the news came on, at which time I became very alert.

It was shortly after twelve when the bedside lamp flicked on and off and then stayed on to inform me that someone was at the front door. I was already dressed and in my stockinged feet so it took me only a few seconds to position myself in the living room beside the doorway to the kitchen and the outside.

I could hear the movement of a key inserted into the lockset and then the latch was released and the door started to swing slowly inside.

I waited till he was halfway through the kitchen before I eased around the corner just enough to be effective but still mostly hidden from his sight. With my left hand I energized, the flashlight, which I focused right in his eyes with the 22 pistol firmly in my right hand.

As I had hoped he had his small Italian hand gun in his hand and we had anticipated as much since he always loved to pack it around and show it off.

As he stood there blinded by the very bright light, I calmly raised my pistol and shot him right through the heart.

As he stood there, swaying, I was beside him in two steps and taking his right hand with the pistol in it. I raised it up and with my finger helping his trigger finger, I fired a shot through the doorway into the living room wall.

As he started to crumble, I stepped to the side and let him fall and watched as he stretched across the kitchen almost to the living room door.

I carefully stepped across the lifeless corpse and switched on the kitchen lights.

Having done this, and ignoring the commotion starting outside I picked up the phone and called the police.

I simply informed them that I had shot an intruder and that he was seemingly dead so there was no hurry and explaining to them that this was a retirement complex, could they please leave their sirens off on the way over.

While waiting for them, I proceeded to shut off the switch for the outside light and then with the power off I proceeded to cut off the extension cord, with the help of side-cutters which I had earlier placed there, a few inches from the outside wall and taping them carefully I pushed the end into the wall and out of sight.

Then I went through the length of the cord and by peeling away the duct tape I recovered it and coiling it I placed neatly in a drawer in my nightstand.

The police were there in under 15 minutes and thank god, no sirens and after a brief look at the situation and the removal of the carcass, I gave them my explanation of the events of the evening.

Unable to sleep I had heard a slight noise from the kitchen. So with gun in hand and with the help of the streetlight shining through the kitchen window, I had observed an intruder with a gun in his hand in the middle of the kitchen.

I had called for him to drop his gun but instead he had raised his gun and fired in my direction.

Fearing my life I had no option but to fire in self-defense and it was not until it was over and I put on the lights, did I realize it was our landlord.

When they questioned the adjoining tenants they were assured by Martha (trouble sleeping) that she was sure she had heard a shout just before the first shot.

The recovery of the spent bullet from Benjie's gun in the living room wall helped corroborate my explanation.

The investigation was short and to the point and interestingly it came out that the police had some suspicions about Benjamin regarding the previous episodes.

The fallout was very satisfying because soon after Benjie's funeral, his widow Moira informed us that when the mortgage was finally done, which would be within six months, there would to be a nice decrease in rents and that improvements were on the way.

Sitting there with Martha and sipping on a nice glass of brandy, we felt comforted that Elizabeth could sleep in peace since justice had finally been done and her murderer had received his proper reward.

# CHAPTER 4

# WRONG HOUSE

There were three of them.

He had been looking out of the window to try to get some idea of the weather outside when he saw the bluish-grey older van come driving slowly down the street.

John Malcom Price and his wife Alice had been living in the same house for thirty-two years, 27 years till his retirement and almost five years since. They loved the house even though it was quite modest as houses go but it had sufficed them very well in the past years when he was working for the municipality and she was raising their family of five. There were only three bedrooms but with a full basement including a fourth bedroom, a second bath and a small rec room and workshop, it had served them well.

The children were gone now on their own working at jobs or with careers with only one of them still in the vicinity, but they all loved to cone home whenever they could with their partners and the grandchildren, especially because the house was at the end of the road on a large lot with a fine garden and privacy and fun for the young ones. It was not unusual for people to drive down to the cul-de-sac just past the house and park for awhile, but there was something about the van and the passengers which caused John some ap prehension.

It was not unusual for people to drive down to the cul-de-sac just past the house and park for awhile, but there was something about the van and the passengers which caused John some ap prehension. It wasn't anything specific but it just didn't feel right, so he watched it for awhile as well as he could through the curtains in the living room till soon it was too dark to see much since there were no street lights on that short street.

It wasn't anything specific but it just didn't feel right, so he watched it for awhile as well as he could through the curtains in the living room till soon it was too dark to see much since there were no street lights on that short street.

After watching the evening news for awhile, he glanced out again and seeing nothing thought, hopefully, that maybe they were through resting and had n1oved on.

It was shortly before 7 p.m. and while they were waiting to finish watching the news before going to have their supper that John was sure ho heard a strange noise by the front door.

They were sitting there quietly trying to figure out what it could be when they heard the sound of breaking glass from the outside basement door. Almost immediately with a great smash, the front door caved inward propelled by a small timber in the hands of two men who came charging into the room to confront John and Alice.

The first one in was not only 6 feet plus, but with his large shoulders and larger gut must have been pushing 300 pounds. The other fellow was of average build and looked to be of mixed nationalities although which one prevailed was hard to tell. Fatso had in his hands a softball bat and with that strange look on his face he was scary to behold. The other fellow, who they soon learned was called Cheemo, appeared unarmed but it seemed he was the wild one.

Throughout this all they could hear the loud thumping of someone charging up the stairs and apparently after smashing the window in the basement door and releasing the lock he was there to reinforce the team.

It became quickly clear to John that these were people who needed money for 1nore drugs and were prepared to take whatever actions that were necessary in order to obtain some.

It soon became obvious that the tall thin fellow who had come up the stairs, he with the hunting knife, Spike, as the others called him, was the main man.

After herding their prisoners into the kitchen area the boys started a quick search of the rooms and soon had dragged out from the bedroom a small cabinet safe that the couple kept there for storing a few bucks and mainly the wife's jewelry which she was planning to leave to her grand daughters.

The combination was quickly forthcoming with John hoping they would grab the loot and go.

His hopes were short lived because the first thing Cheemo did was proceed to drag Alice back into the bedroom, smashing her sharply on the side of the head when she did not immediately comply.

Meanwhile, Spike and Fatso had cracked open a bottle of brandy which they had found in the cupboards and were proceeding to make themselves at home.

With thoughts running through John's mind of other instances where hooligans had broken into senior's residences and after robbing them had so severely beaten then1 that some had died, he be came concerned that these three would hesitate to leave behind two live witnesses who could identify them and cause them jail time.

His thoughts went to his workshop where in his homemade gun cabinet there was a 22 caliber rifle and a clip on the shelf loaded with high powered bullets.

Well, with the knowledge that God hates a coward and Since Spike and Fatso were so enjoying their drinks that they were not paying too much attention to him, he turned and in three steps was at the door to the basement and flinging it open he started down.

He had only managed to negotiate a couple of steps when Spike, hunting knife in hand, was up from his chair and after him. With the difference of age and dexterity between them it was a given that Spike would catch him before he reached the bottom of the stairs.

But the lifesaver to John was that he knew the house well and now it became his ally. Halfway down the stairs there was a cracked thread and Alice had been harping at him for months now to fix it before someone broke their neck because of it.

Since it was fall and no visitors were expect ed for awhile, he had procrastinated and so the fault in the thread was still there. Having to use the stairs on a regular basis he had for his own protection, started counting the steps. He had noticed that as a rule, when he and other people started down that stairway they would use their left foot for the first step down so that it worked out that his right foot only hit the even steps, 2, 4, 6, 8, 10, etc.

Knowing that the dangerous step was number 7 he stepped on number 6 and then swung his body flat against the wall on his right and had his left foot land on step number eight.

Spike, hurrying behind, in an effort to catch his intended victim, and having no idea what was in store, landed with all his weight on number 7. The excessive pressure caused number 7 to collapse, forcing Spikes body sharply to the left whore, glancing off the ➜ left wall, he as John had hoped, just brushed past him on his way down the stairs. Spike, in full flight, landed on the basement floor which, though it had a thin carpet on it, was still concrete and provided a massive blow to Spikes face and head as he landed head first onto it.

As John was stepping over Spikes inert body he noticed that Spike's knife had fallen out of his hand and lay a foot or so beyond him. Thinking "no time like the present", John reached out taking the knife and with all his strength plunged the knife into Spike's exposed neck till it was buried to the hilt.

With the help of the wall, he managed to raise himself upright and then three or four steps and he was through the door of his workshop with the gun cabinet saying hello to him.

It was a simple cabinet he had built himself and not being concerned about beauty he had used good plywood so that it was safe from children. The hasp on the side was meaningless and there was no lock in it, but the gun was secure because it took a firm adult finger to reach to the top right hand corner and press down decisively to release the hidden catch.

As he reached in, removing the gun, and slipping the clip into it, he could hear Fatso hollering excitedly from upstairs, "What in hell is going on down there?" As John stepped into the basement hallway after first levering a bullet into the chamber, and ignoring Spikes intermittent twitching and strange gurgling sounds, he proceeded to the stairs.

He was only a couple of feet from the stairs when suddenly Fatso appeared at the top menacingly waving his bat.

John lifted the rifle and fired, the bullet striking Fatso in the middle of his chest. He stood there teetering for a few seconds before slowly tilting forward and pitching down the stairway to land almost on top of Spike.

As John was proceeding up the stairs, carefully skirting around Fatso and Spike, he could hear footsteps upstairs and at first thought Cheerno was coming towards him, and then immediately realizing that the steps were of someone on their way out the back door. Obviously Cheemo, not liking the sounds of the commotion, and concerned that the jig was up, was intent on departing the scone and saving his skin.

As John reached the top of the stairs on his way to the back door, he could hear Cheemo on the deck rounding the corner of the house and heading to the roadway.

Despite him trying to hurry, when John got sight of the roadway Cheemo was only several steps from the van which was now parked clos er to the house. With the help of the light from the porch and also the rising moon, there was enough visibility for John to see adequately.

The first bullet caught Cheemo high on the right shoulder and slammed him into the side of the van. The second bullet caught him lower down on the left shoulder and with a long loud sigh he slid down the side of van, his hands clawing at the metal as if he was desperately trying to hold on to the life oozing out of him, till finally he came to rest on the ground, at home with his maker.

Only then could John take the time to go and find Alice who was laying there on the bedroom floor with half of her blouse and bra torn off on her right side softly crying and seemingly in a daze. Down on his knee beside her he gently pulled her clothes back about her and then carefully helped her to sit down on the edge of the bed. Going to their closet he found her good winter jacket and he proceeded to help her get it on.

With the admonition to "relax and I'll be right back", he went to their phone and reaching 911 he left this simple message, " My name is John Price and we had some problems at our house, 927 Woodland Drive. My wife has been hurt so I'm going to take her to Saint Saviors Hospital for care. The police should get down here as soon as possible and take care of the problem."

If the police had arrived soon enough they might have saved Fatso, but with the 111anpower shortage as it was and not realizing the urgency of the situation they did not get there till almost an hour had passed.

Cheemo was dead and Spike had died in the interm and although Fatso was still alive when the ambulance took him to the hospital, he died a couple of hours later from having lost too much blood.

The police seargent found John in the waiting room of the emergency area and despite repeated requests to come down to the station to answer a multitude of questions, he had only one response "I will not go anywhere till I am sure Alice is fine."

It was early next morning when the police finally had John in for questioning and then his basic attitude was "That these criminals broke into our house, intending to rob us and kill us, so we had no choice but to fight back to save our lives."

When questioned about his reason for shooting the last man at the van, John explained "I must have been afraid he was going there to get more weapons so I had to stop him from doing that."

When it was basically over the bottom line between the police and prosecutor was that they could live with John killing the first two, but when he followed the third person, who obviously was only trying to escape, and shot him twice in the back, then we have to draw a line and charge him with at least Manslaughter.

The charges being laid, in due process, the judge at the hearing allowed John to be free on his own reconnaissance with a trial date set for a few months down the road.

John had suggested he would be his own defense but it took no time at all until a young aspiring lawyer offered his services at no cost whatsoever. Aware that with the major publicity there would be at this trial, it would be the finest advertising he could get.

When the news media covered the first episode, John began receiving letters of support, some with money in them. When the news came out that he would have to go to trial the volume increased dramatically.

John and Alice used some of the money to do the necessary repairs and clean up at their home, and then with the remainder he set up a separate account in the local bank.

Since they had already been donating to a foster plan to help needy people throughout parts of the world, they simply set the account up so that these additional funds were transferred there.

During the trial the prosecutor kept hammering at the fact that if we could 1naybe justify the killing of the first two people, there was no reason for killing the third who was only trying to escape and that society is responsible for protecting his rights.

After much see-sawing back and forth, the young (hotshot) lawyer got John on the stand and asked him for his comments and an explanation. When John took the stand he was obviously quite nervous but when he spoke he spoke with sincerity and conviction. He stood there straight and calm and it was obvious to all that he spoke with a clear conscience.

When asked by his counsel for his statement, John proceeded with a quiet resolve and explained it so clearly that anyone should be able to understand the situation.

"We were sitting there, not bothering anyone, not asking of anyone for something we were not entitled to. We were watching the news in a home we had paid for by working hard, and trying to enjoy the quiet possession that had been promised us. These three people smashed into our home, robbed us, terrified us, and I firmly believe that they would have in the end killed us before they left. It was only through the grace of God that we finally gained the upper hand and were able to save our lives. The prosecutor keeps repeatedly referring to protecting the rights of these criminals with a total disregard for the rights of the victims and my opinion which I will defend to my dying day is that when these criminals forcibly break into my home, then they have left their rights outside, on 1ny front porch. Upon entering, against n1y will, through my door they have created a war zone and that in a war zone it is dog eat dog and civil rights are non existent. When these three entered into our home it was not their intent to smother us with kindness, rather, they had no respect for humanity and rights and kindness but were driven by madness and greed and a willingness to destroy anything which got in their path. I believe I have the right to protect myself against these intruders, also I have the right and the responsibility to protect my wife and property from being harmed. Further, I believe that when we see mad dogs running around threatening innocent people we should as protectors of our fellow man and society remove them from our midst and thereby their threat to mankind."

When he had finished his statement he had only one comment, when the prosecutor tried to question him further and that was "I am an old man, I am tired and I have no more to say!"

The judge, in his summation, had only one major piece of advice to the jury, in that they should judge in their minds whether John felt fearful for his life throughout the whole process.

The jury was out less than an hour before coming back with smiles on their faces and a verdict of "not guilty".

A word of advice to those people who would prefer that society and their fellow man should provide the1n with all the necessities for their preferred way of life. Some day they may realize that true happiness is best achieved by the effort you put into trying to do something positive and the satisfaction of accomplishing that no matter to how small a degree.

A word of caution to those of you who are prepared to use force in your efforts to achieve that temporary high:

# CHAPTER 5

# OLD ARTHUR

It must have been a small miracle that ho over spotted the shack at all. If he had not glanced up then, instead of a few seconds sooner or later, he would have missed it completely, for with the soft snow drifting down into his face he had kept his gaze on the painted line on the side of the road.

For a few seconds ho almost believed it to be an illusion, for in a matter of a few stops it was gone from sight. Only after he had taken a few steps back did it reappear and then two more steps and it was lost again.

The narrow visual opening showed some sort of structure a fair distance from the highway. He had been hitchhiking for some time with very little luck, and with darkness falling on the winding uphill road, the prospects seerrled very grim. The chance of possibly finding shelter for the night, from this threatening fall snowstorm was hope reborn.

For Arthur, a few 1nonths shy of his 65th birthday, life left nn1ch to be desired, as at that age and with no trade to qualify him, work was hard to find. In his youth he had been full of fire and passion. He had had his good times. He had many things to look back at with satisfaction. But then there were the lost times, like the girl he almost married. Certainly the emotions were there, and there was no question of the attraction between them. She would have surely provided him with a purpose in life and likely a family to belong to. But life had been too full of exciting things to do, new places to see, new people to meet and before long, the opportunity was gone. A couple of years later, when he finally realized where true happiness lay, he returned home but sadly the girl had given up hope on him and had married someone else.

And now with the chance that a sanctuary could possibly be found, he watched the side of the highway for the access road to the building with hawk-like eyes. When at last it appeared it was so faint that, had he not been looking for it he would surely have missed it completely.

When he finally reached the clearing, he came upon a small cabin set against some trees and seemingly unoccupied. The simple keyed lockset was a minor obstacle for Arthur and his pocketknife, and in moments he had worked the latch back and was inside the building. With the aid of a few matches he could see that the interior contained a combination counter and sink with a small wood-fired cook stove against one outside wall and a couch set in a corner, and an interior door.

Further investigation revealed a small bedroom in the area behind the door just large enough for a medium-sized bed.

Having seen no sign of firewood in the cabin and being cold, damp and tired he proceeded to shed his shoes and jacket. Leaning his trusty cane against the wall by his head, he burrowed under the blankets and proceeded to get warm.

His cane was one, which he had fashioned himself from a piece off the top of a tree that had had a solid branch growing out of the side at just the right angle. His patient carving had created a comfortable grip for his hand which was much larger than normal and the cane when held by the bottom end provided him with a formidable weapon of defense and had convinced 1nany a dog to look for other victims.

He soon drifted off to sleep and he could not be sure what it was that awakened him, whether it was the sound of the car engine or the light from the headlights shining though the small window, but he was on his stockinged feet instantly, very alert. His first thought was that, here he was, trapped, having trespassed, forced his way into another's property and could be jailed. The second, and worse, option was that the owner would force him to leave the shelter and go out into the storm.

In his uncertainty he stood there beside the bed with his cane in his hand and watched to see what would transpire. He could hear the engine die but the lights re1nained on facing the cabin. Then the sound of someone at the door, the person entering the building and finally there was light from a flashlight.

Arthur then discovered that the partition between them was only a single layer of boards, which having dried and shrunk, permitted him to see quite well into the main room through the cracks.

The person made his way to a hanging gas lantern, which he proceeded to prepare and light up. By its revealing brilliance he perceived a middle aged balding man somewhat on the smallish size unlike Arthur's 6'1" frame.

Hanging the lantern back on its hook the man proceeded outside and reappeared a few minutes later carrying a rather large bundle, which he carefully placed on the couch. As he slowly removed a blanket, which had been wrapped around the bundle, Arthur was horrified to see that this bundle was actually a small child, the hands and feet taped with duct tape and a gag taped over the mouth.

Many questions raced through his thoughts until slowly the unbelievable picture began to form in his mind, as he recalled a news broadcast he had overheard while having coffee in a cafe earlier that day.

It seems a nine-year-old girl had vanished from school in a small town a few hundred miles away and there were suspicions that she may have been abducted. Without question this was the girl and her abductor, and then the stark realization hit home that the girl would not be allowed to leave the cabin alive.

The cruel and vicious nature of this outrage so appalled Arthur that he began to be filled with a terrible anger. The thought that, had he made a commitment and married s01neone, this child could possibly be a granddaughter. The certain knowledge that both the child's life and his own rested upon him filled him with an icy calm as this atrocity seemed to blend with the many injustices he himself had faced in his lifetime.

Meanwhile, the pervert had returned from outside and laid a bundle of firewood by the stove, and with the aid of some kindling, soon had a fire crackling in the stove. Thereupon he proceeded to his captive and carefully removed the gag from her mouth. She lay there, hound and helpless, her eyes wide with terror reminding Arthur of the look in the eyes of a deer caught in a car's headlights just before the deadly impact.

Arthur's indecision was resolved when the man, obviously somewhat relaxed, since things seemed to be under control headed for the bedroom, probably to allow some warmth to enter that torture chamber. Arthur was by the door in two easy steps and with a silent prayer on his lips he raised the cane, his hands firmly on the bottom end, and with the heavy top high above his head. The man opened the door swinging it against the wall opposite Arthur and was placing his weight in his right leg in the process of entering the room when the cudgel made contact with his right knee in 1nid-swing. The follow through of the drive could have 1nade Arnold Palmer full of envy.

The destructive force behind the blow contained all the pent up frustrations accumulated throughout the years as well as a call for justice, long overdue for this victim and others past. The knee, unable to withstand the irresistible force, folded backward with a shattering of bone and sinew and the man, half-twisting slammed with his head and shoulders into the opposite wall. As a howl of surprise and pain started to well from the fallen man the cudgel was raised again and again descended this time on the mid thigh of the opposite leg destroying it, along with any threat from the enemy. The first howl of pain soon subsided into a moaning, sniveling sound as numbness took over the fallen foe, Arthur's main concern now was only to liberate the child and reassure her that there was now safety at hand.

Arthur was somewhat surprised at how well this information

was received and that in no time she seemed to relax and become quite calm. His search through the cupboards revealed some canned soup and also some crackers, which he prepared for them, as a lunch. Checking the pockets of the jacket the man had hung on the peg by the outside door, he found the keys to the auto and going outside he was able after a few moments to start the car. Finding the tank almost full he left it idling to warm it up.

He now proceeded to carry the child to the front seat of the now warm vehicle and told her to not worry, but to relax till he returned.

All the while Arthur was starting to realize that this was almost certainly not the perp's first victim and slowly the plan was fanning in his head. Laying the helpless fellow on his side, Arthur delivered his proposal. If the man would write out an accurate description of his crimes and a clear set of instructions on how and where to locate the bodies of the other victims, then in return Arthur would send out an ambulance from the closest town to his aid. The alternative would be that the outside door would be left open leaving the cripple to the elements and the animals. Arthur cautioned him about lying, inferring that he had been trailing him for years and knew much of the details already. Having few options the perp proceeded to provide a believable set of accounts onto a notepad, which Arthur had found in the cabin.

Checking through the man's pocketbook provided Arthur with more than $300 in cash, which he promptly confiscated for expense money.

In the process of storing the confession in the car's glove compartment, he found Maxine, she had told him her name, sound asleep on the seat. On his way out of the cabin he debated closing the outside door to protect the occupant from the dropping temperatures but decided against it. Considering the inability of the legal syste1n to protect victims from their assailants he knew it would only be a matter of time before the criminal would be released and out terrorizing again. This time justice would prevail since he was confident it would take him days to be able to retrace his trail for the police's sake.

He drove slowly and carefully to the highway and before long he felt comfortable enough in the car to relax a bit, but still took his time since he had a precious cargo and he was determined to deliver it intact.

While still over an hour from their destination, Maxine awoke and placing her small hand in his large right hand, which lay between them on the seat, she started to tell him of herself.

She and her grandfather on her mother's side had been very close all her life and when she learned he was terminally ill, she had been devastated. On one of her visits she had alone with him, he had held her close and assured her that whatever happened, he would never be too far away and would always look after her. When she had been kidnapped and stuffed into the trunk of the car, she prayed for her grandpa to help her. She gave his hand a gentle squeeze and her remark brought tears to his eyes.

"He knew he couldn't do it himself, so he sent you instead. Thank you."

He had to slow down considerably till his eyes had cleared.

She was rested enough by now and alert, and was able to direct him upon reaching the outskirts of the town and soon they were parking in front of her home. She continued to hold onto his hand on their way to the front door and producing a key from her jacket pocket she slowly unlocked it.

Upon entering the dimly lit room they had proceeded about halfway through, before her mother who had been resting on the couch awoke and spotting Maxine was up in a flash and across the room, her arms enfolding her daughter. With an expression mixed of wonder and relief they stood there in the room, half-laughing, half crying, hugging each other. Her father, hearing the commotion had wandered out of their bedroom and in an instant they were one con1pact group. Shortly, realizing that this was not just imagination, they managed to separate, whereupon Maxine, letting go of her father and mother came over to Arthur, who had been standing quietly all the while by himself in the corner, and taking a hold of his hands while looking up into his face, said in a soft, but very clear voice, "Guess what Mom, Grandpa's back."

www.ingramcontent.com/pod-product-compliance
Lightning Source LLC
Chambersburg PA
CBHW020522030426
42337CB00011B/513